MARIE ANTOINETTE

A Life From Beginning to End

Table of Contents

Introduction

Marie Antoinette came into this world on November 2, 1755, in Vienna, Austria as Maria Antonia Josepha Johanna. She was born an archduchess, the daughter of Maria Theresa, the empress of the Holy Roman Empire. The Holy Roman Empire was a conglomerate of states in central Europe whose leadership styled themselves to be successors of the ancient Roman Empire. Maria Theresa was already the seated sovereign of the Hapsburg Empire before acquiring the additional title of empress by marrying her husband, Holy Roman Emperor Francis I.

Maria Theresa was a busy woman, and as such, practically as soon as Marie was born she was given a stand-in surrogate mother in the form of a governess named Countess von Brandeis. Countess von Brandeis served as Marie's first caretaker and later instructor. Not a lot is known about the governess except that she was a "kind but simple" woman. One thing that is certain, however, is that Marie Antoinette absolutely adored her first instructor. Unfortunately for her, this love would soon become misplaced, since due to what her mother viewed as Brandeis' constant coddling and lack of discipline with the child, she was removed as caretaker and replaced by a more rigid and stern woman named Countess Lerchenfeld.

Marie Antoinette never ceased to mourn for her old instructor and was slow to warm up to Countess Lerchenfeld. This relationship, which was often at odds, resulted in the continued suffering of Marie Antoinette's education. Her learning was said to be so stunted, in fact, that by the age of ten, she could barely write. The education of royals was not all that rigorous in the latter half of the eighteenth century, but the ability to effectively write letters was considered of the utmost importance, and here Marie seemed to have met with consistent failure. Those who knew her at the time commented on this arrested development, remarking that whenever she took pen to paper it was a laborious task in which she wrote at a "snail's pace," with plenty of blotches and misspellings of words.

Even though she was slow to write, however, Marie Antoinette was not slow to verbally converse with her peers. Under the guidance of court musician Christoph Willibald Gluck, she also became a rather accomplished musician, learning to play the flute, harp, and harpsichord. If she had been allowed to pursue these studies, it is possible that she could have become a skilled composer just like her one-time childhood acquaintance and fellow Austrian—Wolfgang Amadeus Mozart.

But in those days, musical composition was not the craft expected of young princesses; their number one draw was their potential prospects in marriage. And so with her daughter just barely a teenager, Empress Maria Theresa was already looking towards the shores of France for the right prince for her daughter.

Chapter One

Groomed to Become Queen

"It would be doing me great injustice to think that I have any feeling of indifference to my country; I have more reason than anyone to feel, every day of my life, the value of the blood which flows in my veins, and it is only from prudence that at times I abstain from showing how proud I am of it."

—Marie Antoinette

After the sudden death of her husband, Holy Roman Emperor Francis I, on August 18, 1765, Maria Theresa became intensely focused on the marriage prospects of her children. And for Marie Antoinette in particular, she soon found what she thought to be just the right match in the form of the young Prince Louis-Auguste of France. In this marriage she hoped to end the animosity held between the two nations, uniting Austria and France through the marital union of Marie Antoinette and Louis-Auguste.

Louis-Auguste at the time was said to be fairly far from a prince charming, however, with his own relatives referring to him as being "overweight, uncouth, badly dressed and painfully self-conscious." Nevertheless, the marriage was set to go forward for the projected date of April 1770. It is interesting to note that Prince Louis-

Auguste's father, Louis XV, was quick to request full painted portraits of Marie Antoinette's likeness to be sent to his son before the marriage, but no such portraits of Louis-Auguste were forthcoming. Marie Antoinette was seemingly content to be left completely in the dark as to her future husband's appearance until her wedding day. In arranged marriages during this time period, it was actually considered imprudent and unladylike for a woman to question the partner she had been paired with; it was expected of the bride-to-be to place all of her faith and trust in her matchmakers and leave the rest to fate.

As it turns out, Marie's mother finally requested a portrait of the French prince which was hastily sent. Shortly thereafter, an initial wedding ceremony was conducted in Vienna at the Augustinian Church on April 19, 1770. Even though her prince was not in attendance, for the benefit of the Austrian court Marie Antoinette was married by proxy with her brother Archduke Ferdinand taking the place of Prince Louis-Auguste. It is said that Marie Antoinette seemed happy during this occasion of symbolism and smiled pleasantly as her brother slipped the ring onto her finger.

Her good spirits would serve her well for the true journey that she was about to embark upon, in both the metaphorical as well as the literal sense; the physical journey of Marie and her immediate entourage out of the courts of Austria and on toward the Kingdom of France began just two days later. Her impressive caravan carried all of her clothing and favourite artifacts from her ancestral palace.

As her carriage pulled away from the only home she had ever known, it is said that Marie Antoinette took some time to look back. She silently bid the place of her birth goodbye and made herself look forward to the future as her horse-drawn carriage ploughed forward toward its ultimate destination—the Palace of Versailles, in Paris, France. Louis-Auguste, meanwhile, would leave in his own separate entourage and meet her halfway.

The two finally crossed paths in a newly constructed chapel situated on a small island on the Rhine River that separated Germany from France. Although many of his peers viewed him with contempt, when Marie Antoinette laid eyes on her soon-to-be husband for the first time, she saw many of the same defects but also what she viewed to be a gentle soul. She saw his timidity and was stirred to render him aid.

The flawed prince actually managed to stir the fires of compassion within Marie Antoinette, and she felt that perhaps this disheveled heir to the throne—with her help—could be shaped into a respectable figure after all. Whether she was consciously aware of it or not, from the very beginning, Marie Antoinette was positioning herself to become the leading authority of France. And as the courtesans of Louis began to realize the future that was taking shape, they began to engage in backbiting and all manner of connivances against the young Marie Antoinette.

The official Versailles wedding for the pair was held on May 16, 1770. It was an extravagant affair with thousands of onlookers in attendance. From the beginning, every movement of the bride and groom were watched very carefully, including the ritual bedding ceremony in which the king gave Prince Louis-Auguste his night shirt. Marie Antoinette and her ladies in waiting meanwhile went to another room to help prepare her for bed.

Once in bed, with the door to the bedchamber shut, the two were quite thankful that this is where the voyeurism of the French public came to an end and they were finally left to enjoy what was left of their honeymoon. Alone with her new prince, Marie Antoinette had been both eagerly anticipating and fearing this moment of union since her engagement to Louis-Auguste had begun. Her mother had attempted to prepare 14-year-old Marie with what to expect on her wedding night, but her motherly guidance seemed to fall somewhat short when Louis-Auguste simply rolled over and went to sleep.

Chapter Two

The Failed Wedding Night and Political Intrigue

"We made our entrance into Paris. As for honors, we received all that we could possibly imagine; but they, though very well in their way, were not what touched me most. What was really affecting was the tenderness and earnestness of the poor people, who, in spite of the taxes with which they are overwhelmed, were transported with joy at seeing us."

—Marie Antoinette

Soon after her wedding, the blushing bride Marie Antoinette was mortified to find that she was the number one topic of conversation among the rumor mills of Paris, France. And the biggest conversation piece was the apparent lack of consummation of her marriage. Even though no one was openly speaking of such intimate details, the truth seemed to get out due to the investigative prowess of a few maidservants who took it upon themselves to examine the bedclothes of Marie Antoinette.

It was due to the observations from the domestic help that the tell-tale signs of blood were conspicuously absent from the sheets and clothing of Marie Antoinette that the idea began to be floated that perhaps that there was something amiss with the intimacy of this new royal marriage. It wasn't long before it was being whispered about that the French prince was impotent, or perhaps he simply didn't care for his new bride. But neither of these was the case. As it turns out, Prince Louis had a condition called phimosis in which the foreskin of his uncircumcised penis failed to retract properly, thereby causing any attempt at intimacy to be difficult and extremely painful. The shy prince had unsurprisingly never broached such a sensitive topic with anyone, both due to his own timidity with discussing such matters and in his knowledge that doing so would result in a painful trip to the court doctor for corrective surgery.

Despite their lack of intimacy, the friendship between the prince and princess had grown, and Marie had begun to build up an increasingly impressive power base. This foundation would serve her well on May 10, 1774 when the reigning French King Louis XV abruptly died, making Louis-Auguste thereafter take on the mantle of King Louis XVI, and Marie Antoinette the title of Queen of France.

But no matter how many friends she made, and how much of a socialite she became in royal circles, Marie knew all too well that if she was not able to produce an heir, she could easily lose her place and position at Versailles. This was the direct warning that her brother and then emperor of the Holy Roman Empire Joseph gave her when he paid a surprise visit to the courts of Paris in April of 1777. At this point, Marie Antoinette was twenty-one years old and had been married to Louis for seven years, three of those years as queen, without any sign of pregnancy. Since it was Marie Antoinette's number one duty to the state to produce an heir, the situation was considered intolerable.

The ensuing scandal from the odd circumstances of Marie Antoinette's marriage had now reached such a fever pitch in Europe that the elder brother felt he had no choice but to intervene. Arriving under the alias of Count Falkenstein, and posing as a nobleman rather than emperor, he sought to get to the bottom of the matter that was afflicting the married couple as discreetly as he possibly could. It was after a few private, yet blatantly candid conversations with the two, that Joseph discovered the bad case of phimosis that was hindering the newly crowned King Louis.

He found that Louis had by this time actually brokered the topic of corrective surgery with his physicians, but after discussion both sides fearfully backed out; one for his fear of personal pain and the others for fear of the guillotine should they botch the surgery. Joseph managed to persuade the king to move forward with the operation, and shortly after his departure, King Louis's phimosis was finally corrected. Eight months later, the queen was pregnant.

France meanwhile became embroiled in matters of international intrigue when Marie's brother attempted to take hold of the throne of Bavaria. Joseph II, head of the Holy Roman Empire had invaded the realm in January of 1778, and the move was immediately opposed by

Frederick II, the king of Prussia, who threatened war if Joseph did not immediately remove his army from the region. Predictably enough, in the face of this threat, Joseph immediately sought the aid of his sister, Queen Marie Antoinette.

But Marie could not convince her reluctant husband to intercede on Joseph's behalf. It seems that even though he felt greatly indebted to this brother-in-law for helping to bring about a cure for his phimosis, King Louis XVI was still not too keen on getting involved. Marie was amazed to find just how insistent her usually compliant husband was with his policy of non-interference. At one point, in the midst of her pleading, the king told his wife rather bluntly, "Your relatives' ambition will upset everything. I am very sorry for you." King Louis was disgusted with his brother-in-law Joseph's political maneuvering, but he still felt remorse for the position that it had placed Marie in. And when Frederick II made good on his threats and sent an army to invade Austria in July 1778, Marie Antoinette was found crying hysterically, and wishing that she could, "mingle her tears with those of her mother."

In May 1779, the crisis finally came to a close with the signing of the Peace of Teschen. Even though she couldn't prevent the conflict, Marie proved to play a major role in the war's conclusion as mediator. With her intervention she managed to allow Austria to gain extraterritorial acquisitions consisting of some 100,000 people. It was this intervention that would forever cast suspicion among the French people that Marie Antoinette was nothing more than an Austrian transplant with deep sympathy for her homeland and nothing but treachery for France. Fairly or unfairly being cast in such light, Marie Antoinette would spend the rest of her days attempting to get out from under it.

Chapter Three

The American Revolution and the Birth of a King

"My dear mamma is quite right when she says that we must lay down principles and not depart from them. The king will not have the same weaknesses as his grandfather. I hope that he will have no favorites; but I am afraid that he is too mild and too easy. You may depend upon it that I will not draw the King into any great expenses."

—Marie Antoinette

Growing up in Austria Marie Antoinette probably never imagined that the private affair of giving birth to her first child would be on public display. But as she went into labor on December 19, 1778, hundreds of curious French crowded in and around her bedchambers to bear witness to the event. In France it had long been tradition to have a public viewing of royal births so that no one could question who the rightful mother of the child was after the fact.

It is said that shortly after the birth of her first-born Marie Antoinette collapsed and fell into a fitful sleep. It was while she was unconscious that the court physician determined the sex of the child. It is said that upon regaining consciousness and being informed that she was the mother of a baby girl, Marie let out a shriek of disappointment, since it was her desire as reigning queen to produce a male heir to the throne. She soon came around to her young daughter, however, and when the child was presented to her recovering mother, Marie held her close to her person as she lovingly whispered, "Poor little thing, you are not what was desired, but you shall not be less dear to me. A son would have belonged more particularly to the state. [But] you will be mine; you will receive all my care; you will share all my happiness and soothe my sorrows."

In tribute to her mother, Marie Antoinette named her Marie-Thérèse, demonstrating her wish for the same strong maternal bond that she had enjoyed with her own mother. The girl's father, King Louis XVI, is said to have been even more doting, absolutely enthralled by his child, giving her every attention he possibly could.

But in the midst of all of the couple's adulation for their firstborn, events on the world stage would soon break through their revelry. The American Revolution that had erupted in 1775 was now in its third year. Early on, the French had sought to secretly aid the Americans against their arch nemesis the British by delivering arms and other strategic aid. But beyond this tacit support, the French were not yet willing to take sides in the conflict. Then in late 1777, the Americans had shown surprising resolve and against all odds had managed to give the British a resounding defeat in the Battle of Saratoga. This was enough to convince the French to side with the

Americans officially. It was shortly after this victory that France recognized the United States of America as an independent nation—the first country to do so.

Louis XVI then took France even further into the orbit of the United States by signing an official military alliance with the Americans on March 13, 1778. Ever since coming out on the losing end of the Seven Years' War in 1763 which saw France losing huge territories in North America, many in the French government were looking for a way to get back at the British. And supporting the American rebellion against the British Empire seemed the perfect way to do so. Never mind the seemingly incompatible ideological nature of a French absolute monarch supporting the democratic overthrow of monarchical control, Louis XVI didn't need much convincing to throw his lot in with the Americans.

King Louis was soon receiving important American leaders such as Benjamin Franklin directly in his courts to discuss the progress of the struggle against the British. Marie Antoinette herself had become fascinated with the events taking place in America and was sure to assert her opinions as they unfolded. She was particularly pleased toward the end of the war when her mother, Empress Maria Theresa, decided to offer her hand in mediating a peace agreement between England and France. Such notions would ultimately be quashed, however, when the empress abruptly passed away on November 29, 1780, at the age of 63. Upon hearing the news, it is said that Marie was immediately overcome with grief; the death of her mother would be one of the saddest moments of her life.

The war would then officially end three years later in September of 1783 with the Americans and the French victorious against the British. And with the ratification of the so-called Treaty of Paris signed in the city of the same name between representatives of all parties, the gains of France were laid out for all to see. In particular, France was allowed to regain much of the territory in America, Africa, and India that it had lost in the Seven Years' War just a few decades prior.

But even though France seemed to have come out on top at the conclusion of this conflict, the rapidly rising debt that had been accumulated—about three billion livres—was now sinking the nation. It was a heavy burden for King Louis and Marie Antoinette to sort through, but their financial troubles were at least buoyed by the birth at long last of a male heir to the French throne. On October 22, 1781, Marie Antoinette gave birth to a son named Louis Joseph Xavier Francois. It was on this young heir's shoulders that the future of the entire kingdom would rest.

Chapter Four

Madame Deficit

"In order to deal justly and equitably with your subjects, be straightforward and firm, turning neither to the right hand nor to the left, but always following what is just, and upholding the cause of the poor till the truth be made clear."

—Louis XI

By all accounts, during the first decade of their marriage the royal couple had been exclusively loyal to each other, shunning the notion of extramarital adventure. But in 1783 when a dashing veteran of the American revolution—the Swedish nobleman and adventurer—Count Axel von Fersen arrived at Versailles, all that was about to change. Axel and Marie had met previously and were always on close terms, but now he became an intimate associate in the queen's inner circle, and as it has long been alleged, he also became her lover.

The nature of Marie Antoinette's relationship with the count has long been debated, but some believe that the affair was finally proven without a shadow of a doubt in 2016 when researchers announced special x-ray scanners were able to read long indecipherable letters, in which the romantic liaison between the two was openly discussed. It seems that twenty-first-century science has lent some credence to the gossip peddlers of eighteenth-century France after all.

At any rate, von Fersen managed to secure a position as commander of the Royal Swedish Regiment—a special infantry unit of the French army composed exclusively of foreign troops. This position would allow the count to routinely travel back and forth between his home in Sweden and the courts of Marie Antoinette, making him a regular fixture in her life. This relationship certainly didn't help Marie Antoinette's image with the public, and soon regular pamphlets were being produced depicting the queen in all manner of compromising positions with the count and many other members of the French court.

It is said that that the Palais Royal regularly sold this kind of smutty literature slandering the queen and accusing her of all manner of crimes and debasements of her role in office. Besides depicting the queen as adulterous, the other main vein of accusation that these pamphlets promoted was that Marie Antoinette was an unrepentant squanderer of French money. And in 1783 when Marie determined to create her own personal palace in the countryside, for many it seemed to be proof that the accusations of the gossip columns were correct in their assertions. She was further ridiculed for the particular design of this extravagance.

The queen apparently wished to recreate the feel of a rural village and had engineers construct several small thatch-roofed cottages, which although brand new were purposefully constructed to look old, complete with cracks and weathered paint. Marie wished to simulate the simple life of the average French citizen, and in doing so she provoked both their ire and their laughter. The queen was widely lambasted at having attempted to "create a village for her own amusement while in many parts of France real peasants in real villages were in dire want."

This whimsical simulation of the peasantry attached to the queen's new country estate seemed to encapsulate the general feeling of the populace—that Marie Antoinette was hopelessly out of touch with her subjects and was bankrupting the nation for her own capricious whims. Even though the land was largely purchased from sales of other royal properties, the perceived extravagance soon earned her the nickname "Madame Deficit" under the belief that Marie Antoinette was recklessly adding to the already substantial deficit in the French economy. The queen became increasingly viewed as a waster and reckless spender, who viewed the common citizen as nothing more than a quaint backdrop and an object for her own amusement.

But as bad as her reputation was becoming, the worst was still in store. It all began in the summer of 1785 when a certain cardinal of the Church and regular scoundrel of the world named Louis Rene Edouard de Rohan sought to gain the queen's affections. At the time, Rohan was in his fifties and yet had a reputation as a womanizer and was actively seeking to seduce Marie Antoinette with his charms.

Marie would have nothing of it though and consistently gave him the cold shoulder any time they crossed paths. Rohan, who was quite used to having his way with women, was none too pleased and was attempting to find a way to remedy the situation when he became acquainted with a woman named Jeanne de Saint-Remy, who claimed to be a personal acquaintance of the queen. Then, through subsequent conniving and conning, she managed to convince the cardinal that she knew just how to gain the queen's admiration.

Through elaborate deceit, Jeanne managed to trick the cardinal into obtaining a diamond necklace worth an astounding 1.6 million livre. She told him that the queen wished to purchase the jewelry and put him up to obtain it from the jeweler. The royal jeweler, upon hearing Rohan repeat Jeanne's claim that the queen was backing the acquisition, readily handed over the necklace in the good faith that the queen would pay for it. Rohan then handed the necklace off to Jeanne who pretended that she was going to hand it over to Marie Antoinette but in reality gave it to her husband who fled to England to fence the merchandise.

Marie herself found out about the scam when she received notice from the jeweler that he was expecting payment for a necklace she had never purchased. The unfortunate Rohan was then immediately seized and delivered to the king's ministers to face questioning. Although the royal wrath initially fell squarely on Rohan's shoulders, interrogation revealed that Rohan had been a dupe of Jeanne de Saint-Remy. The cardinal was arrested for the conspiracy nevertheless and Jeanne, believed to be the mastermind of the plot, was taken into custody the next day.

During the course of their trial, the French public became increasingly divided as to who held the blame for the incident. Many believed that Rohan was just a patsy tricked into carrying out the crime, and Jeanne was the true miscreant. But those that harbored a previous dislike of the cardinal weren't so ready to absolve him of wrongdoing. Among these divided sentiments, however, there appeared to be a common thread, with the vast majority somehow blaming Marie for the scandal, even though she had nothing to do with it.

And to add to her dismay, in May of 1786 Rohan— who she felt should be found guilty of fraud—was found not guilty. It was determined that Jeanne de Saint-Remy would shoulder all the blame for the debacle and was promptly found guilty and sent off to prison. But no matter the verdict, it was all bad publicity of the worst kind for the queen, and she would forever be associated with an exorbitantly expensive necklace that she had never even worn.

Chapter Five

The Roots of Revolution

"Every time that I fill a high office, I create a hundred discontented men and an ingrate."

—Louis XIV

Despite the royal couple's best efforts to be frugal and curtail expenses, the French economy continued to stall as the national deficit increased. At the urging of Charles Alexandre de Calonne, the minister of finance, King Louis soon called an Assembly of Notables, the first session of which was held on February 22, 1787. Marie Antoinette was conspicuously absent, and her lack of participation served to fuel gossip that she was unconcerned and perpetually apathetic about the state of the French economy.

The notables themselves did not amount to much and were unwilling to consider the reforms offered by Finance Minister Calonne, forcing the minister to resign. King Louis XVI seemed to blame all of the economic woes of France on the failures of his finance minister to come up with a cohesive strategy. On one occasion with Marie Antoinette he had raged, "That scoundrel—Calonne! I should have had him hanged!" But the removal of Calonne did little to help the situation.

His replacement, an archbishop named Étienne Charles de Loménie de Brienne, had sought to remedy the problem by curtailing spending at court, but all of these efforts were too little too late. In the end Brienne's efforts could not fix the burgeoning deficit, and by May 25, the Assembly of Notables was completely disbanded due to the stagnation of government. Financial matters were not going to improve on their own, however, and as the French economy continued to take a nosedive, King Louis ordered all of the members of the Paris Parliament to assemble for a Royal Session at Versailles.

Here, the king sought to get the representatives to sign off on a new edict that would allow the royal office to take out a loan of some 440 million livres in order to avoid a complete government shutdown. Considering how desperately the funds were needed to keep even the most basic of governmental apparatuses functioning, King Louis figured that members of Parliament would readily agree to the measure. He was wrong.

Instead, as soon as the new measures were introduced, an intense debate was ignited between representatives. This volatile back and forth would last for an astounding seven-hour discussion. The king sat and helplessly listened to the bickering until he finally had enough. Seeking to circumvent the traditional protocol, he decided to unilaterally issue the edict on his own without the approval of Parliament. But as soon as the frustrated king made his intention known, none other than his cousin, the duke of Orleans, shouted from across the room at him that what he intended to do was illegal.

Upon hearing this affront from the duke, King Louis XVI, about to lose his composure completely, jumped out of his seat and screamed, "I don't care!" before storming out of the building. Such actions only played right into the hands of those who claimed that the king was a tyrant and that the royal family of France behaved as if they were above the law. In the end, the cause of all of this dysfunction would inevitably go back to the French public's favorite scapegoat, the transplanted queen from Austria—Marie Antoinette.

Marie, now the mother of four, had a full house of her own to deal with. Her oldest son Louis-Joseph faced a series of medical ailments as well as a severe deformity of the spine that left him perpetually crippled and hunched over. These ailments culminated in his untimely death on June 4, 1789, at the age of seven. Marie Antoinette, who had placed all of her hopes for the future on Louis-Joseph's diminutive shoulders was understandably beside herself with grief, unable to focus on much else but the tragic loss.

But tumultuous events in Paris would soon cut even this traumatic grief short. The frequent protests against her and the regime had now taken on an altogether more volatile caste, and the sporadic demonstrations had become highly organized events. The authorities had long given up attempting to control the roving bands, and now they were being directed by vocal agitators and professional inciters of mob violence to do their worst to the ruling elite of France. Rather than controlling the rioters, in many cases soldiers joined their cause.

Things had gotten so bad that the only parts of the army that King Louis could effectively depend upon were the German and Swiss regiments. These troops were far enough removed from the daily drama and gossip of Paris not to be compromised by the disloyal bent that had taken hold of so many others that were stationed in France. Battalions of these troops were gathered together under the command of an old French veteran, Marshal de Broglie, who was ordered to bring back order to the streets of Paris.

But King Louis himself, wishing to project a benevolent image to the people that hated him so much, requested that the old general show restraint in corralling the rioters. Wishing to prove to those who shouted from the rooftops that he was nothing but a tyrannical monarch that they were wrong, King Louis XVI wanted to avoid the shedding of blood as much as possible. This order of restraint, however, would serve as a direct handicap to the cause of bringing law and order back to the streets. In one of those strange irony's that history is full of, in King Louis's attempts to appease the mob, he merely quickened his own demise.

Chapter Six

Storming of the Bastille

"When the government violates the people's rights,
insurrection is, for the people and for each portion of the
people, the most sacred of the rights and the most
indispensable of duties."

—Marquis de Lafayette

While the streets of Paris fell into complete chaos with the citizens running riot over the bankrupt economy, those closest to King Louis XVI urged him to act. He was advised that he needed to quell the unrest with a strong show of force in order to show the people of France that he was still in charge. But King Louis saw things differently; he believed that unbridled force leading to bloodshed would only stoke further public outrage against him. Instead, he determined that it would be better to wait out the crisis until public emotion settled down and cooler heads prevailed.

As he told his advisers at the time, "To resist at this moment would be to expose the monarchy to peril; it would lose us all. I have retracted my orders; our troops will quit Paris. I shall employ gentler means. Do not speak to me about a coup d'autorité, a mighty act of force. I believe it more prudent to temporize, to yield to the storm, and above all to bide my time, for the awakening of the men of good will and the love of the French for their King." Unfortunately for Louis, he would be left waiting for such reasoned sentiment to prevail—and would not see it again in his lifetime.

In fact, his restrained, gentle approach had the opposite effect on the populace; instead of giving them space to calm down, the lack of immediate repercussions for their riotous actions merely emboldened them to riot even further. If a mob of peasants saw that they could smash open the windows of a bakery and take all the bread without fear of arrest, it served as a direct incentive to do so again. It was a rather simple calculus, but the king failed to see the formula that was at work. The less he pushed back against those who wished to destroy him, the more they marched toward his utter destruction.

In addition to bread, the rioters frantically searched for a means to arm themselves. On July 14, 1789, the swelled ranks of revolutionary rebels took over the Hôtel des Invalides—a hospital for wounded veterans. The roving bands of protesters knew that they could find weapons at this depot and overwhelmed the facility, demanding that all guns be given up. The director of the facility initially attempted to refuse, but being surrounded he soon had no choice but to acquiesce, and the group stormed past him to retrieve armaments that were being stored in the cellar. In all the rebels retrieved 28,000 muskets and 10 cannons.

But even though these revolutionaries had made a major find, there was a slight problem; there was not much ammunition or gunpowder in store. Without ammunition and gunpowder, the weapons were useless. It was then pointed out that the Bastille, an ancient fortress turned prison, was said to house a large amount of ammunition. So it was that this group of rag-tag rebels was fated to storm into the Bastille on July 14, 1789. It seemed to the revolutionaries that the taking of this dreaded symbol of the royal family would be the perfect coup for the rebellion. Not only would they gain the proper armament needed for a full-scale revolution, but it was also believed that the Bastille housed political prisoners languishing in the dark dungeons of the fortress. It was now a rallying cry for the rioters to break into the Bastille, arm themselves, and free those who were suffering under the tyranny of the royal family.

As the rebels gathered around the Bastille, the defenders, no doubt keeping in mind the king's wish for restraint, were initially hesitant to open fire. They aimed their cannons at the riotous crowd but did not immediately act. It was only when the group managed to force down the outer drawbridge and gain access to the building that they finally began to discharge their weapons into the crowd. Now shots were being fired on all sides, and both attacking rebels and fortress defenders began to lose their lives in the onslaught.

After the skirmish was initiated, wishing to end the carnage, the Bastille's governor of operations, a man named Bernard-René Jourdan de Launay, soon decided to capitulate to the attackers and ordered his men to stand down to allow the rebels access. It's not clear if the governor thought that he could immediately switch sides to the cause of the revolution by such an act, but his efforts would not be rewarded. Despite his capitulation, the attackers held a grudge against the governor and blamed him directly for the deaths of their fellow rebels during the attack. And as soon as de Launay was in sight, he was viciously attacked, murdered, and his corpse desecrated.

It was an unbridled rage that took over the revolutionaries, and in that moment all of their pent-up aggression with the status quo of French society found a release on the unfortunate governor as his dead body was repeatedly shot and stabbed by the marauders. It wasn't enough to kill such a person; the maddened mob wished to see him suffer further indignity after his death. And even as rigor mortis was beginning to set in, someone shouted, "His head! Cut off his head!" Sadly enough, this "off with his head" kind of mentality would come to permeate the whole revolution, and soon dreadful scenes such as this would be repeatedly perpetuated all throughout France.

After the storming of the Bastille, the invaders managed to get their arms and free a handful of prisoners (contrary to popular belief, the dungeons were nearly empty at the time), but this dramatic event would go on to symbolize much more. It would come to embody the spirit of unbridled rage, the madness without conclusion that was getting ready to send an entire nation into complete chaos.

Chapter Seven

Under the Protection of Lafayette

"Defender of the liberty that I idolize, myself more free than anyone, in coming as a friend to offer my services to this intriguing republic, I bring to it only my frankness and my good will; no ambition, no self-interest, in working for my glory, I work for their happiness."

—Marquis de Lafayette

In the aftermath of the storming of the Bastille, a steady stream of nobility and aristocrats began to evacuate France for more hospitable terrain. King Louis and Queen Marie Antoinette soon began to contemplate whether or not they should join them. The king, as indecisive as ever, left the decision up to his handlers, asking his ministers what they believed to be the best course of action. The majority of these officials argued that it would be too dangerous to leave all at once; for the moment it would be safer for them to stay where they were.

Marie Antoinette adamantly disagreed with this assessment, however, and felt that they and their entourage should relocate to the north, in the much more stable environs of Metz, France. The queen argued that from there the king could consolidate the forces that were still loyal to him and then use the army to recover any territory lost to the rebels. But for once, King Louis XVI, often accused of being controlled by Marie Antoinette, refused to listen to the words of his wife and instead followed the advice of his ministers and decided to stay put. Nevertheless, even after this last-ditch decision was made, Marie Antoinette held on to her gut feeling that they were making a mistake and began to pack all of their possessions in anticipation that they would soon have to flee for their lives.

On July 17, 1789, the king made the startling announcement that he would personally make the trip back to Paris to address the National Assembly. Marie Antoinette was certain that her husband would be killed, but King Louis, believing until the end that his people would never actually do him harm, was bravely determined to soldier on. He was accompanied by only 12 bodyguards and a small armed guard from Versailles. Upon his arrival, it had been pre-planned for the king's entourage to be intercepted by General Gilbert du Motier, Marquis de Lafayette. Known as the "Hero of Two Worlds," Lafayette had played an integral role in the American Revolution, and now that he was back on French soil he was attempting to assert his authority in yet another popular uprising of the people.

Lafayette now had the strange role of being the champion of revolution and yet at the same time having the obligation to protect the king. It was only the power of Lafayette that kept the mobs of French citizenry from attacking the king's entourage and seizing the monarch by force. As it were, King Louis was distressed to see throngs of armed masses on every corner. Every step his procession took towards the National Assembly was followed closely by thousands of men, women, and even children, who were all heavily armed. They carried guns, swords, and even improvised weapons such as sickles, scythes, and chisels.

The king, nevertheless, arrived at his destination unharmed and settled himself in for a long night of speeches and eventually made his way to the podium to make a speech of his own in which he agreed that reform and certain concession needed to be made. At this moment, boldly addressing his fiercest critics without fear, King Louis managed to vindicate himself of much of the lifelong claims of his timidity. When the speech was over he even adorned his hat with the tri-color ribbon symbolic of the revolution, as if to tell the crowd that he was indeed on their side. Incredibly, the masses of people who previously wanted nothing more than the king removed from power, imprisoned, or worse began to cheer their sovereign on with shouts of, "Vive le Roi!" or as it were, "Long live the King!"

King Louis then left shortly thereafter, making his journey back to Versailles as if he were on a triumphal march, reassured that he was right after all to wait on the good will of the people. But this gesture of admiration directed at him from the masses would be short-lived. Soon after his return from Versailles, King Louis would receive word that massive revolts had broken out in cities all over France, proving that the contagion of the French Revolution was not being contained to Paris but had spread like wildfire all across the country. City officials linked to the old regime were being systematically removed from power and replaced with revolutionary governments modeled after the post-revolution municipal government that had been created in Paris.

The National Assembly too, was on the move, with legislation created on August 4, 1789 making the historic decision of abolishing feudal rights tied to the land, instantaneously scrapping centuries-old economic practice with the signing of a pen. Then on August 26, the Assembly further solidified its grip on the course of the new direction of the nation, by drafting the Declaration of the Rights of Man and the Citizen. Heavily inspired by the American Declaration of Independence, this document was meant to ensure the "inalienable rights" of all French citizens.

But even more pertinent to the royal family was the passage of the document seemingly directed toward them that declared that government existed for the benefit of the governed and not to benefit those who govern— meaning King Louis and Queen Marie Antoinette. This meant that no longer would a French figurehead reap any benefit at the expense of the French citizenry.

Life for Marie Antoinette and her family at the palace was getting more and more dire by the day. There were constant threats, and the palace had become full of revolutionary spies and informants watching every move and reporting them back to their handlers. It seemed that any hope of escape from the nightmare that they had found themselves trapped in was gone. Lafayette, the head of the National Guard, was now in charge of protecting the palace. But it often seemed as though their protectors were more like their jailers, making sure that they were trapped and unable to extricate themselves from the terrible situation that they were in.

Chapter Eight

Women's March on Versailles

"I had displeased the Jacobins by blaming their aristocratic usurpation of legitimate powers; the priests of all sorts by claiming religious liberty; the anarchists by repressing them; and the conspirators by rejecting their offers."

—Marquis de Lafayette

As the summer of 1789 turned into autumn, the food crisis in Paris had become even worse. The starving populace began to once again amass in the streets chanting for bread. Then on October 5, 1789, a massive armed mob with hundreds of women at the lead began marching toward Versailles shouting that the king should stop hiding at the palace and return to his capital to tend to his starving people.

The hundreds of women who led the way, waving their brooms, pitchforks, and knives were the most vocal, screaming violent chants such as, "Hang the Queen, and tear her guts out!" and "How shall we divide her up?" followed by responses such as, "I'd like to rip her belly open and tear out her heart!" and "I'll have a leg!" or the ever popular, "I'll eat the innards!" It seems like something out of a horror movie, but this was the reality of the French Revolution, in which the worst inclinations of humanity were allowed to flourish. It was a rag-tag group that marched on the palace to be sure, but they were still far too numerous for the beleaguered royal bodyguard to handle on their own.

General Lafayette and the National Guard that was supposed to protect the palace merely followed closely behind the mob without engaging them. Lafayette, who was courting favor with revolutionaries in high power, was apparently afraid to risk his own standing by engaging the rioters in open combat. Lafayette and his troops finally arrived at King Louis's side shortly before midnight and assured the king that he and his men would see to the safety of the royal family.

But despite his pledge of overseeing their protection, shortly after he uttered the words, Lafayette left the palace grounds and retired for the night. The rioters meanwhile had camped out just outside the palace gates, in what had become a kind of macabre festival filled with all manner of obscenity and violent desire. And as they drank, cavorted with one another, and shot off muskets, they continued to sing and chant their desires to cannibalize the royal family.

For most of the night, the massive gates had managed to keep the murderous crowd out, but then right around the break of dawn, one of the gates that Lafayette's troops were supposed to be guarding inexplicably opened. Most historians have since concurred that the gate could not have opened unless through the express treachery of these guards. Soon the rioters were pouring into the palace grounds shouting louder than ever their intent to maim and massacre. They came upon the entrance to the royal staircase and found two royal guards in place standing watch. These two men were obviously no match for the mob before them, but they courageously stood their ground nonetheless.

Incredibly, these two men were able to temporarily hold back the hundreds of rebels who assailed them, but it was only a matter of time before they were cut down. One was almost immediately stabbed to death, while the other managed to keep his back to the stairs, and slowly back up to his comrades above as he methodically parried a multitude of blows. He was able to alert his fellow guards to barricade the doors before succumbing to his wounds. This guard was then replaced by others, who were cut down in defense of the staircase as well. The last guard to perish in this manner managed to shout and alert the queen's maids who were nearby to get the queen to safety, as he exclaimed that the "tigers with whom he was struggling were aiming at her [Marie Antoinette's] life."

It was around 4:30 in the morning when this notice was given, and Marie Antoinette was in a deep sleep brought on by severe exhaustion. Her maidservants were able to rouse her, however, shouting, "Get up, madame—don't stay to dress yourself, fly to the King's apartments!" They pleaded with Marie to flee for her life to the safety of King Louis chamber before her bedroom was overrun with the blood-thirsty horde. The rooms were adjoined by locked doors, and after pounding on one of them she was able to get a servant from the king's chambers to let her inside.

It was soon after the royal family took refuge in the king's chambers that Lafayette finally made a return appearance and managed to wedge his troops between the attackers and the royal family. With momentary safety assured, King Louis went out to the balcony to see if he could somehow talk sense to the crowd. But the maddened citizenry drowned out his words by shouting, "The Queen! The Queen!" Answering the twisted call for her to make an appearance, Marie Antoinette then stepped out to join her husband. Upon seeing her, the crowd expressed their apparent desire to have the queen singled out by shouting, "No King. No children". And incredibly enough, King Louis obliged them by having he and his children return to the chambers, leaving Marie Antoinette to fend for herself in front of the crowd below.

As she stared out at her audience, they began to scream obscenities at her such as, "There she is, the damned whore!" and "We want her head, never mind the body!" Despite such violent vitriol being hurled at her, Marie Antoinette was able to stoically address those assembled, and apparently impressed with her overall demeanor, the crowd grew silent. Marie Antoinette then gave a slight curtsy which managed to evoke a few shouts of, "Vive la Reine!" or as it is in English, "Long live the Queen!" The crowd that had wanted to rip her limb from limb and eat her innards just seconds before were now wishing her to have a long life. Such bizarre shows of changes of heart seemed to be an endemic side effect of the revolution.

The very next thing the crowd began to chant was not murder but "To Paris! To Paris!" This was apparently their way of expressing their desire to have the royal family escorted back to Paris so that they could "look after them." Upon hearing this, King Louis returned to the balcony and responded accordingly, "My children, you want me to follow you to Paris. I consent, but on condition that I shall never separate from my wife and children." But of course, with hundreds of rioters standing right outside his window, the king was certainly in no position to cut deals or make conditions.

Chapter Nine

The Last French King and Queen

"Terror is only justice; prompt, severe and inflexible; it is then an emanation of virtue; it is less a distinct principle than a natural consequence of the general principle of democracy, applied to the most pressing wants of the country."

—Maximilien Robespierre

It was a bizarre scene, the royal caravan being led back to Paris flocked by hundreds of dirty, blood-stained, and half-naked rioters dancing and singing in drunken revelry. Many in the French countryside were understandably shocked at what they were witnessing, but the ragged revolutionaries as they passed them by had a simple message for them. Their cry of triumph to whoever they encountered was, "Cheer up friends. We no longer have to be in want of bread; we bring you the baker, the baker's wife, and the little baker boy!" This was of course in reference to King Louis, Queen Marie Antoinette, and their one surviving son, the heir apparent to the throne.

The rioters herded their prized prisoners into the Tuileries Palace in Paris where they would remain under the guard of Lafayette's army. Here they would stay, until on June 21, 1791, after much dithering and delay, Marie Antoinette and her husband King Louis finally made plans for an escape. The plot entailed the royal family being disguised as servants while the governess of the children posed as a rich Russian baroness. But the disguised family only made it as far as the French town of Varennes; shortly before midnight they were arrested after they failed to produce proper passports.

The entourage had been stopped by National Guardsmen and questioned about who they were and where they were going. Attempting to play the roles that they had given themselves, the governess, posing as Russian royalty shouted back at their interrogators that she was the Baroness de Korff and that they were in a hurry. The guards demanded to see her passport, which she readily handed over. The guards then ordered them to stay put as they went into the Inn to observe the document by candlelight.

When the guards returned, they informed the group that the passport did indeed check out but insisted that the baroness and her companions remain with them for a period of 24 hours so that they could all be accounted for. The group now had no choice but to stay at Varennes. A short time later, the guard came back to them with a local judge who had once resided at Versailles and was quite familiar with the royal family's likeness. The judge apparently was not one to forget a face, because as soon as he saw King Louis, he knelt down on his knee and shouted, "Oh, sire!" exposing the royal family for who they really were.

Weary of the ruse and feeling denial would be futile anyway, King Louis sighed, "Yes—I am indeed your King. These are my wife and my children. We beg you to treat us with the regard which the French have always had for their King." The family was then escorted back to Paris where they were once again placed under armed guard. Here they languished in a tormented limbo. But their condition would soon deteriorate even further when France declared war on Austria on April 20, of 1792. After a series of defeats at the hands of the Austrians, Marie Antoinette became once again a target because of her Austrian ancestry and was accused of delivering military secrets to the enemy.

On September 21, 1792, the monarchy was declared to be officially abolished, and former King Louis XVI was hauled into court to face charges of "undermining the First French Republic." Louis was found guilty and was ultimately executed on January 21, 1793. Marie Antoinette was terribly grieved by the loss but still held onto the hope that perhaps her lone surviving son would one day be able to succeed his father on the throne and lead the nation. But the French Reign of Terror had only just begun.

Conclusion

The dark epoch of French history known as the Reign of Terror erupted in the summer of 1793 in which a new instrument of execution, the guillotine, was put into heavy use decimating perceived enemies of the state. Radicals, revolutionaries, and self-proclaimed intellectuals who all felt they knew how society should be run were eager to decimate anyone they felt were a threat to their vision. Marie Antoinette would face the steel of the guillotine's blade after she was tried and convicted of treason in October of that same year.

Marie Antoinette was accused of treason for passing state secrets and money to Austrian agents. Even more startling, she was also accused of committing incest with her surviving son. It was the latter charge that provoked a response from the otherwise stoic queen, who balked in outrage at the absurd claims being promoted in the courtroom. But there was no way that she could win in this court, and on October 16, 1793, she was found guilty and was executed shortly thereafter. It was a sad end for a woman who had traveled so far in life only to be felled by those so close to her.

Made in the USA
Monee, IL
20 December 2019